A Publication of the Emergency Management Work Group

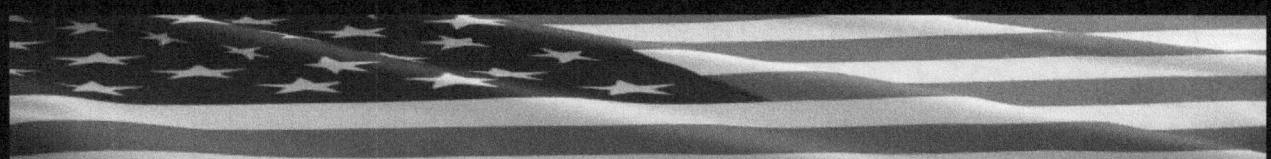

An IG's Guide for Assessing Federal Response Capabilities

August 2010

Council of the
INSPECTORS GENERAL
on INTEGRITY and EFFICIENCY

The Council of the Inspectors General on Integrity and Efficiency

The Council of the Inspectors General on Integrity and Efficiency (CIGIE) was statutorily established as an independent entity within the executive branch by the *"Inspector General Reform Act of 2008," P.L. 110-409.* The mission of the CIGIE is to:

- Address integrity, economy, and effectiveness issues that transcend individual government agencies; and
- Increase the professionalism and effectiveness of personnel by developing policies, standards, and approaches to aid in the establishment of a well-trained and highly skilled workforce in the Federal Inspectors General (IG) community.

The CIGIE Homeland Security Roundtable

The CIGIE Homeland Security Roundtable was formed after the establishment of the Department of Homeland Security (DHS) to share information and identify best practices relating to homeland security oversight operations. The Roundtable participates on an ad hoc basis with various external organizations and governmental entities regarding the performance of agency programs and operations that impact homeland security. Also, after Hurricane Katrina, the Homeland Security Roundtable created the Emergency Management Work Group (EMWG), which is comprised of representatives from various Federal IG offices. The EMWG meets quarterly to prepare for disaster-related oversight and to collaborate on oversight when a disaster occurs. The group's goals are to provide: (1) leadership to the IG community in the area of oversight for emergency management; (2) a forum for all participating IG offices to share information, ideas, and strategies regarding oversight activities designed to reduce fraud, waste, and abuse, as well as enhance emergency management operations; and, (3) an environment that will foster collaboration and mutual development of skills and abilities in emergency management oversight.

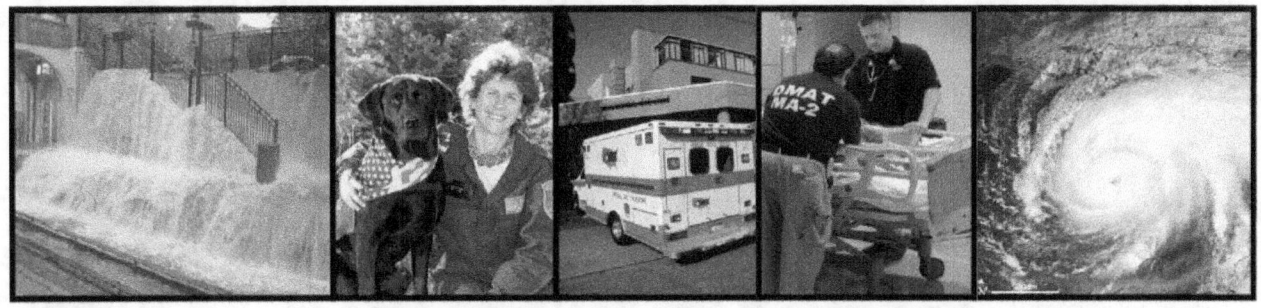

PREFACE

The *National Response Framework* emphasizes the importance of engaged partnerships in the effort to enhance our Nation's preparedness to respond to domestic threats and disasters both natural and manmade. Leaders at all levels of government must communicate and actively support engaged partnerships to develop shared goals and align capabilities so that none allows the other to be overwhelmed in times of crisis. Each governmental level plays a prominent role in developing the capabilities needed to respond to incidents to include developing plans, conducting assessments and exercises, providing and directing resources and capabilities, and identifying lessons learned and acting upon them. These activities require that organizations understand their roles and responsibilities and how they fit within and are supported by the *National Response Framework*.

.The Federal government maintains a wide array of capabilities and resources that can be made available in response to a disaster. No fewer than 12 Federal departments and agencies have key ESF roles and responsibilities outlined in the *National Response Framework*. When an incident occurs that exceeds local and State resources, the Federal government uses the *National Response Framework* to involve all necessary department and agency capabilities, organize the response and ensure coordination with response partners. The overarching objective of response activities centers upon saving lives and protecting property.

By conducting independent assessments and offering recommendations that will enhance response readiness, IG offices play a vital role in advancing emergency response capabilities for their respective department or agency. A forward-leaning Federal posture is imperative for incidents that have the potential to expand rapidly in size, scope or complexity, and for no-notice events. Developed by the EMWG, this *Guide* can be used by the IG community to assess the response capabilities of their respective department or agency. The criteria for this *Guide* are based on ESF roles and responsibilities of Federal departments' and agencies' designated Coordinator, Primary Agency, and Support Agency, pertinent to each ESF.

Contents

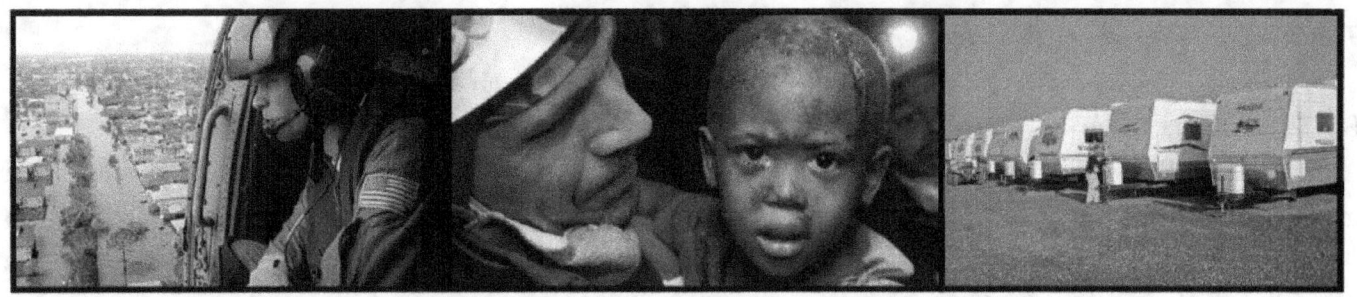

I. Fostering Federal Response Preparedness: What You Need To Know Before You Begin

In August 2005, Hurricane Katrina made landfall on the southern coast of the United States with devastating effects. Hurricane Katrina's powerful winds, storm surge, and subsequent flooding destroyed communities and infrastructure along the Gulf Coast. The storm also inflicted a terrible toll of human suffering, killing at least 1,330 and injuring thousands.

Hurricane Katrina exposed deficiencies in the Federal government's ability to respond to a catastrophic disaster. In February 2006, the White House released its examination of the failed Federal response to Hurricane Katrina. The report concluded, "Insufficient planning, training, and interagency coordination are not problems that began and ended with Hurricane Katrina. The storm demonstrated the need for greater integration and synchronization of preparedness efforts, not only throughout the Federal government, but also with the State and local governments and the private and non-profit sectors as well."[1]

Eight months later, Congress enacted the *Post-Katrina Emergency Management Reform Act of 2006* to address the shortcomings identified in the preparation for and response to Hurricane Katrina.

Hurricane Katrina just prior to landfall in August 2005.
Source: The National Oceanic and Atmospheric Administration

The legislation charged the Federal Emergency Management Agency (FEMA) with leading the Nation's efforts to prepare for, protect against, respond to, recover from, and mitigate the risk of natural disasters, acts of terrorism, and other manmade disasters, including catastrophic incidents. It also provided that the FEMA Administrator may develop, in coordination with the heads of appropriate Federal agencies and the FEMA National Advisory Council, planning scenarios that reflect the relative risk requirements presented by all hazards.

---

[1] White House Report, *The Federal Response to Hurricane Katrina: Lessons Learned*; pg. 50.

The National Planning Scenarios

DHS released the *National Preparedness Guidelines* in September 2007 to define what it means for the Nation to be prepared for all hazards. A critical element of the *National Preparedness Guidelines* is the National Planning Scenarios.

The National Planning Scenarios, which were developed by the Homeland Security Council in partnership with Federal departments and agencies and State, local, tribal, and territorial governments, depict a diverse set of credible, high-consequence threat scenarios regarding both potential terrorist attacks and natural disasters. Table 1 is a listing of the 15 National Planning Scenarios presented in the *National Preparedness Guidelines*.

Table 1: The National Planning Scenarios

(1) Improvised Nuclear Device	(9) Major Earthquake
(2) Aerosol Anthrax	(10) Major Hurricane
(3) Pandemic Influenza	(11) Radiological Dispersal Device
(4) Plague	(12) Improvised Explosive Device
(5) Blister Agent	(13) Food Contamination
(6) Toxic Industrial Chemicals	(14) Foreign Animal Disease
(7) Nerve Agent	(15) Cyber Attack
(8) Chlorine Tank Explosion	

These scenarios are designed to focus contingency planning for homeland security preparedness work at all levels of government and with the private sector. Appendix A provides an overview of each of the 15 National Planning Scenarios.

The National Response Framework

The *National Response Framework* was released in January 2008 and is intended to be the guide to how the Nation conducts all-hazards response. It is built upon a scalable, flexible, and adaptable coordinating structure to align key roles and responsibilities across the Nation, linking all levels of government, nongovernmental organizations, and the private sector. It includes specific authorities and best practices for managing incidents that range from the serious but purely local, to large scale terrorist attacks or catastrophic disasters. It underscores that government executives, private-sector and nongovernmental organization leaders, and emergency management practitioners across the Nation must understand domestic incident response roles, responsibilities, and relationships.

The Emergency Support Function Annexes

The ESF Annexes to the *National Response Framework* provide the structure for coordinating Federal interagency support in response to an incident. They represent 15 functional groupings that are frequently used to provide Federal support to States and Federal-to-Federal support, both for

Officials from the Federal Emergency Management Agency (FEMA) and the National Oceanic and Atmospheric Administration (NOAA) meet at FEMA's National Response Coordination Center to mark the onset of the 2010 National Hurricane Preparedness Week.

Source: FEMA Photo Library

declared disasters and emergencies under the Stafford Act and for non-Stafford Act incidents. Table 2 is a listing of the ESFs and corresponding Federal Coordinator and Primary Agency for each. Appendix B provides an overview of each ESF.

Each ESF is comprised of a Coordinator, along with Primary and Support Agencies. The Coordinator for each ESF is charged with management oversight for that particular ESF. The Coordinator has ongoing responsibilities throughout the preparedness, response, and recovery phases of incident management. Responsibilities of the ESF Coordinator include:

- Coordination before, during, and after an incident, including pre-incident planning and coordination.

- Maintaining ongoing contact with ESF Primary and Support Agencies.

- Conducting periodic ESF meetings and conference calls.

- Coordinating efforts with corresponding private-sector organizations.

- Coordinating ESF activities relating to catastrophic incident planning and critical infrastructure preparedness, as appropriate.

An ESF Primary Agency is a Federal agency with significant authorities, roles, resources, or capabilities for a particular function within an ESF. A Federal agency designated as an ESF Primary Agency serves as a Federal executive agent under the Federal Coordinating Officer or Federal Resource Coordinator to accomplish the ESF mission. When an ESF is activated in response to an incident, the Primary Agency is responsible for:

- Supporting the ESF Coordinator and coordinating closely with the other Primary and Support Agencies.

- Orchestrating Federal support within their functional area for an affected State.

- Providing staff for the operations functions at fixed and field facilities.

- Notifying and requesting assistance from Support Agencies.

- Managing mission assignments and coordinating with Support Agencies, as well as appropriate State officials, operations centers, and agencies.

- Working with appropriate private-sector organizations to maximize use of all available resources.

- Supporting and keeping other ESFs and

organizational elements informed of ESF operational priorities and activities.

- Conducting situational and periodic readiness assessments.

- Executing contracts and procuring goods and services as needed.

- Ensuring financial and property accountability for ESF activities.

- Planning for short- and long-term incident management and recovery operations.

- Maintaining trained personnel to support interagency emergency response and support teams.

- Identifying new equipment or capabilities required to prevent or respond to new or emerging threats and hazards, or to improve the ability to address existing threats.

A Support Agency is an entity that has specific capabilities or resources that support the Primary Agency in executing the ESF mission. When an ESF is activated, a Support Agency is responsible for:

- Conducting operations, when requested by DHS or the designated ESF Primary Agency, consistent with their own authority and resources, except as directed otherwise pursuant to sections 402, 403, and 502 of the Stafford Act.

- Participating in planning for short- and long-term incident management and recovery operations and the development of supporting

operational plans, Standard Operating Procedures, checklists, or other job aids, in concert with existing first-responder standards.

- Assisting in the conduct of situational assessments.

- Furnishing available personnel, equipment, or other resource support as requested by DHS or the ESF Primary Agency.

- Providing input to periodic readiness assessments.

- Maintaining trained personnel to support interagency emergency response and support teams.

- Identifying new equipment or capabilities required to prevent or respond to new or emerging threats and hazards, or to improve the ability to address existing threats.

Table 2: ESFs and Corresponding Federal Department or Agency

ESF	ESF Coordinator (C)/Primary Agency (P)
ESF-1 Transportation	Department of Transportation (C/P)
ESF-2 Communication	DHS/National Communications System (C/P)
ESF-3 Public Works and Engineering	Department of Defense/U.S. Army Corps of Engineers (C/P)
ESF-4 Firefighting	Department of Agriculture/Forest Service (C/P)
ESF-5 Emergency Management	DHS/FEMA (C/P)
ESF-6 Mass Care	DHS/FEMA (C/P)
ESF-7 Logistics	DHS/FEMA (C/P) General Services Administration (C/P)
ESF-8 Public Health	Department of Health and Human Services (C/P)
ESF-9 Search and Rescue	DHS/FEMA (C/P) Department of Defense (P) DHS/U.S. Coast Guard (P) Department of the Interior (P)
ESF-10 Oil and Hazardous Materials Response	Environmental Protection Agency (C/P) DHS/U.S. Coast Guard (P)
ESF-11 Agriculture and Natural Resources	Department of Agriculture (C/P) Department of the Interior (P)
ESF-12 Energy	Department of Energy (C/P)
ESF-13 Public Safety and Security	Department of Justice (C/P)
ESF-14 Long-Term Community Recovery	DHS/FEMA (C/P) DHS (P) Department of Agriculture (P) Department of Housing and Urban Development (P) Small Business Administration (P)
ESF-15 External Affairs	DHS (C) DHS/FEMA (P)

II. Evaluating Your Agency's Emergency Response Capabilities

Each ESF Annex in the *National Response Framework* identifies the Coordinator and the Primary and Support Agencies pertinent to the ESF. Several ESFs incorporate multiple components, with Primary Agencies designated for each component to facilitate the seamless integration of and transition between preparedness, response, and recovery activities. To assess a department or agency's response capabilities, we developed researchable questions based on the specific ESF roles and responsibilities of the Coordinator, Primary Agency, and Support Agency. Appendix C contains the corresponding Inspection Matrix for this *Guide*. Appendix D provides a listing of internet resources that can be helpful in executing your review.

The researchable questions pertaining to the ESF Coordinator are:

- To what extent and in what manner do you coordinate with other ESF Coordinators, Primary and Support Agencies (a) before an incident (including pre-incident planning), (b) during an incident, and (c) after an incident?

- To what extent do you coordinate with private sector organizations to identify and maximize use of private sector resources in response to a threat or incident?

- To what extent do you coordinate ESF activities for catastrophic incident planning?

The researchable questions pertaining to the ESF Primary Agency are:

- To what extent and in what manner do you coordinate with the ESF Coordinator, Primary and Support Agencies, State officials, operations centers, State agencies, and the private sector?

- To what extent are you prepared to provide trained staff for operations functions, such as supporting interagency emergency response and support teams, at fixed and field facilities?

- To what extent and in what manner do you conduct situational and periodic readiness assessments? How often have they been coordinated, and how have findings been applied?

- To what extent have you identified new equipment or capabilities required to prevent or respond to new or emerging threats and hazards, or to improve the ability to address existing threats?

- To what extent have you executed contracts and procured goods and services needed to fulfill your ESF role?

- To what extent are you prepared to manage mission assignments and ensure financial and property accountability for ESF activities?

- To what extent do you plan for short- and long-term incident management and recovery operations?

The researchable questions for the ESF Support Agency are:

- To what extent have you identified trained personnel, equipment, or other resource support to conduct operations when requested by DHS or the designated ESF Primary Agency?

- To what extent do you participate in planning for short- and long-term incident management and recovery operations and the development of supporting operational plans?

- To what extent do you assist in the conduct of situational assessments and provide input to periodic readiness assessments? How often have they been coordinated, and how have findings been applied?

- To what extent do you identify new equipment or capabilities required to prevent or respond to new or emerging threats and hazards, or to improve the ability to address existing threats?

Lessons Learned from Piloting the Guide

During the pilot of the *Guide*, we identified some tips that could improve the efficacy of your review.

During or immediately following the entrance conference, provide the department or agency being reviewed a document request that outlines what evidence is needed to respond to each researchable question. If possible, provide an example of a document you know the agency has developed that represents sufficient evidence for a particular question. For example, Standard Operating Procedures for an ESF developed in collaboration with the primary and support agencies would demonstrate ESF coordination before an incident.

Prior to conducting interviews, consider providing the department or agency official being interviewed the interview questions in appropriate circumstances. This may help ensure the official is fully prepared for the interview and is given the opportunity to respond to the questions in writing. This can be helpful when linking the written response to document support during the work paper preparation process.

Work closely with the IG Liaison within the agency if appropriate to schedule the entrance conference and facilitate interviews to ensure all personnel with ESF roles and responsibilities are identified and appropriate personnel are interviewed.

Prior to conducting interviews, a survey to identify existing issues can help in determining specific areas that can be of concern. For example, a review of after action reports can provide the reviewer with an understanding of previous or ongoing issues.

III. Afterword: Understanding Your Critical Role

The failed Federal response to Hurricane Katrina highlighted the importance of disaster preparedness and demonstrated what happens when a Nation fails to integrate preparedness activities among all stakeholders. The White House's report on the failed Federal response to Hurricane Katrina concluded: "Hurricane Katrina necessitated a national response that Federal, State, and local officials were unprepared to provide...The Federal response suffered from significant organization and coordination problems during this week of crisis." [2]

The Government Accountability Office reported in April 2009 that FEMA efforts on the national preparedness system are lacking.[3] The report determined that nearly 4 years since Hurricane Katrina, FEMA has failed to clarify the responsibilities of different agencies that would respond to such disasters. DHS said, in response to the report, that it generally concurs with the recommendations and is already taking steps to improve but added that because FEMA lacks authority over other Federal agencies and departments or State and local governments, it is unfair to expect the agency to compel compliance with the national preparedness system. Speaking in

May 2009, FEMA Administrator Craig Fugate underscored the importance of all stakeholders being prepared to respond to a threat or disaster: "One thing I want to make clear is FEMA is not the team...FEMA is a part of the team."

Enhancing the Nation's preparedness cannot rest on the shoulders of one department or agency. Rather, we are all partners in the Nation's attempt to ensure that we are prepared the next time tragedy strikes. Our Nation's ability to withstand the next catastrophe will depend on our coordinated efforts to identify and strengthen our capabilities and readiness. Unity of effort among all responders is indispensable to all incident response activities and requires a clear understanding of the roles and responsibilities of each participating Federal department or agency. We in the IG community play an important role in ensuring that our department or agency is fully engaged and prepared to respond to the next crisis, whatever it may be. We trust this *Guide* will be helpful in this endeavor.

---

[2] White House Report, *The Federal Response to Hurricane Katrina: Lessons Learned;* pg. 50.

[3] GAO-09-369, April 30, 2009, *National Preparedness: FEMA Has Made Progress, but Needs to Complete and Integrate Planning, Exercise, and Assessment Efforts.*

Appendices

Appendix A

National Planning Scenarios Overview[4]

Scenario 1: Nuclear Detonation – Improvised Nuclear Device

Members of a terrorist organization have detonated a 10-kiloton improvised nuclear device in a heavily populated metropolitan area. The initial detonation causes total infrastructure damage in a 3-mile radius and various levels of radiation spanning out 3,000 square miles. As casualties climb in excess of several hundred thousand, hundreds of thousands of survivors either shelter in place or are forced onto the city's transportation system to seek shelter in safe areas or evacuate the city. The city is now facing hundreds of billions of dollars in damage and a recovery effort that will take years.

Scenario 2: Biological Attack – Aerosol Anthrax

Two individuals release 100 liters of aerosolized anthrax into the air of a major metropolitan city. More than 330,000 people are exposed to the anthrax spores. Casualties and injuries resulting from the inhaled anthrax and subsequent infection reach upwards of 13,000 people. The economic costs associated with the closure and decontamination of affected areas may run in the billions of dollars,

and the city will likely face a recovery effort that will take months.

Scenario 3: Biological Disease Outbreak – Pandemic Influenza

A new strain of avian influenza has spread to the United States. Estimates predict that fatalities could range anywhere between 209,000 and 1.9 million people, with an even greater number requiring hospitalization. Hospital bills alone could reach upwards of $180 billion.

Scenario 4: Biological Attack – Pneumonic Plague

Members of a terrorist organization manufacture the causative agent of plague and disseminate it in several metropolitan areas using biological warfare dissemination devices. Approximately 36 hours after release, patients begin showing up at hospitals with rapidly progressing and severe respiratory illnesses. Estimates predict that fatalities could range upwards of 9,500 people with approximately 28,383 people becoming ill. As word gets out that pneumonic plague is spreading, hospitals will see an influx of people crowding into emergency rooms, possibly creating a shortage of available beds.

Scenario 5: Chemical Attack – Blister Agent

Members of a terrorist organization use a lightweight aircraft to spray Agent Yellow, which is a mixture of two blister agents that can cause permanent damage to the respiratory system if inhaled

[4] *National Planning Scenarios,* Version 21.3. Final Draft, March 2006

and severe burns to the eyes or skin, into a crowded college football stadium. Thousands are injured and many are killed as people flee from the contaminated scene. Additional injuries and fatalities will occur as a result of contact with the blister agent. Tens of thousands of people will need decontamination, as well as both short-term and long-term care.

Scenario 6: Chemical Attack – Toxic Industrial Chemicals

Sleeper cells of a domestic terrorist organization have launched a multiphase attack at a port and a nearby petroleum refinery. Utilizing vehicle-borne improvised explosive devices, the terrorists target a U.S. Coast Guard facility and two container ships containing hazardous material. The terrorists initiate the second phase of the attack by launching rocket-propelled grenades into the center of the petroleum refinery. Several hundred people are killed, thousands are injured, and thousands more are forced to evacuate or shelter in place as a result of the explosions, fires, and vapor plume. Recovery efforts will likely take months and the economic impact will likely be in the billions.

Scenario 7: Chemical Attack – Nerve Agent

Members of a terrorist organization have acquired the nerve agent sarin and have released it into the ventilation system of a large office building in a metropolitan area. The agent quickly kills 95% of

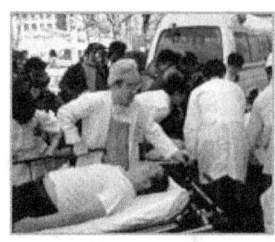

the building's 6,000 occupants. Even more injuries and deaths occur as first responders arrive on the scene unaware of the current conditions. As the nerve agent escapes the building, almost 50,000 people located in adjacent buildings are forced to shelter in place. Recovery time will likely be 3 to 4 months, with the total economic impact reaching upwards of $300 million.

Scenario 8: Chemical Attack – Chlorine Tank Explosion

Members of a terrorist organization have detonated an explosive device on a 60,000-gallon storage tank filled with liquefied chlorine gas. The terrorists have also planted improvised explosive devices, set to detonate at varying intervals, close to the tank in order to harm emergency responders. Within an hour, there are almost 10,000 people crowding into emergency rooms with severe respiratory difficulties. As the gas continues to move downwind, as many as 35,000 people, or 5% of those in the affected area, are exposed to potentially lethal doses of chlorine gas. Recovery will take several weeks and likely cost millions of dollars.

Scenario 9: Natural Disaster – Major Earthquake

A major metropolitan area, with a population of almost 10 million people, experiences a 7.5 magnitude earthquake followed shortly by an 8.0 magnitude earthquake. In the area within 25 miles of the fault, many homes and buildings are completely destroyed. Approximately 1,400 people are killed, 100,000 more are crowding into hospital emergency rooms, and an intense search and rescue for an estimated 20,000 people has been launched. Recovery efforts are expected to range from several months to several years, and the estimated total economic impact is projected to be in the billions.

Scenario 10: Natural Disaster – Major Hurricane

A category 5 hurricane, with sustained wind speeds in excess of 160 miles per hour and a storm surge 20 feet higher than normal, makes landfall at a major metropolitan area. The storm surge, heavy winds, and subsequent tornados spawned by the hurricane cause destruction to nearly 200,000 homes and result in nearly 1,000 fatalities. With such a wide path of destruction, recovery from the hur-

ricane will likely take several months to a couple of years with the total economic impact reaching into the billions.

Scenario 11: Radiological Attack – Radiological Dispersal Devices

Members of a terrorist organization have manufactured and detonated a radiological dispersal device or a "dirty bomb" in three regionally close, moderate to large cities. Each explosion causes significant damage to many of the buildings and structures in the immediate area of the blast. At each site, there are approximately 180 deaths and upwards of 20,000 detectable contaminations. Recovery efforts will likely take several months to a couple of years. Total economic loss will be in the billions.

Scenario 12: Explosives Attack – Improvised Explosive Device

Members of a terrorist organization have carried out a multipronged attack using improvised explosive devices at a large urban entertainment/sports venue. Three suicide bombers detonated their devices, killing and injuring some people and sending the rest of the large crowd in a frantic rush to the exits, where they are met by the detonation of a large vehicle bomb. Similar detonations also occur near a crowded public transportation concourse, a parking lot, and inside the lobby of the nearest hospital emergency room. The explosions combine to cause millions of dollars in damage and to kill approximately 100 people. Recovery efforts will take weeks.

Scenario 13: Biological Attack – Food Contamination

A member of a terrorist organization, who works at a meat processing plant on the West Coast, contaminates the meat with anthrax. Two contaminated batches of ground beef were sent to two different States. In a 10-day span, hospitals on the West Coast begin to see a sudden influx of people with gastrointestinal problems. Upwards of 1,800 have become ill and there have been 500 fatalities.

Recovery efforts to address contamination sites and provide for those who have become ill will take millions of dollars and likely last for several weeks.

Scenario 14: Biological Attack – Foreign Animal Disease

Members of a terrorist organization have launched a biological attack on the agricultural industry by infecting livestock at various transportation sites with a foreign animal disease. Farmers in several States quickly realize that many of their animals are ill. As it is realized that a foreign animal disease is spreading, recovery efforts will likely take weeks and require hundreds of millions of dollars to diagnose, quarantine, destroy, and dispose of livestock.

Scenario 15: Cyber Attack

Members of a terrorist organization launch a cyber attack against critical infrastructures that rely on the Internet. Service disruptions occur across many sectors and there is a general fear that there will be a loss of confidence in the Internet and the services it provides. Recovery efforts will likely take months and cost upwards of several hundred million dollars.

Emergency Support Function Overview

ESF-1: Transportation

ESF-1 helps Federal, State, tribal, and local governments and nongovernmental organizations manage transportation systems and infrastructure in the wake of a major incident. Coordinated by the Department of Transportation, ESF-1 aids communities in the immediate aftermath and recovery phase of a catastrophic event. Working in coordination with ESF-1 Support Agencies, the Department of Transportation: (1) monitors and reports on the condition of damaged transportation systems and infrastructure; (2) coordinates temporary alternative solutions whenever systems or infrastructure are damaged, unavailable, or overwhelmed; and, (3) performs activities conducted under the direct authority of the Department of Transportation operating administrations. Once the immediate danger has subsided, ESF-1 helps recovery efforts by coordinating the restoration and recovery of the transportation infrastructure and by working with the Department of Homeland Security to support prevention, preparedness, and mitigation activities among all transportation stakeholders.

ESF-2: Communication

ESF-2 supports the restoration of the communications infrastructure, facilitates the recovery of systems and applications for cyber attacks, and coordinates Federal communications support to response efforts. Coordinated by DHS' National Communications System, ESF-2 also provides communications support to Federal, State, and local governments and first responders with access to repair communications infrastructure, security to protect responders and equipment, and fuel to support communications in absence of commercial power. In addition to coordinating ESF-2 activities, the National Communications System serves as the Primary Agency for the restoration of telecommunications in an incident area, and FEMA acts as the ESF-2 Primary Agency for the support of public safety disaster emergency communications.

ESF-3: Public Works and Engineering

ESF-3, under the coordination of the Department of Defense's U.S. Army Corps of Engineers, provides the immediate support that State and local governments will need in the aftermath of a major disaster to provide basic necessities, such as electricity, secure shelters, drinking water, and safe transportation routes. As the ESF-3 Coordinator and Primary Agency for response, the U.S. Army Corps of Engineers, along with ESF-3 Support Agencies, assist State and local governments by: (1) constructing emergency access routes; (2) providing temporary emergency power to critical facilities and providing potable water and sanitation; (3) demolishing damaged structures and conducting debris removal and disposal; and 4) conducting post-incident damage assessments to determine critical needs and potential workloads.

As the immediate response begins to subside, FEMA, serving as the Primary Agency for recovery, guides the long-term recovery effort. FEMA directs the Federal government's recovery programs that repair, replace, or relocate damaged or destroyed facilities and infrastructure.

ESF-4: Firefighting

ESF-4, coordinated by the U.S. Department of Agriculture's Forest Service, provides Federal support for the detection and suppression of wildland, rural, and urban fires resulting from, or occurring coincidently with, an incident requiring a coordinated Federal response. The Forest Service and the ESF-4 Support Agencies form a firefighting system that consists of highly trained and experienced personnel. The Forest Service assumes responsibility for the suppression of wildfires on national forest system lands, provides and coordinates firefighting assistance with other Federal, State, and local fire organizations, and works directly with fire officials to coordinate requests for firefighting assistance in structural or industrial fires.

ESF-5: Emergency Management

ESF-5 serves as the coordination ESF for all Federal departments and agencies across the spectrum of domestic incident management from hazard mitigation and preparedness to response and recovery. Serving as the ESF-5 Coordinator, as well as the Primary Agency, FEMA: (1) conducts operational and strategic planning; (2) activates and convenes Federal emergency assets and capabilities; (3) coordinates Federal preparedness, response, recovery, and mitigation planning activities; (4) coordinates the use of remote sensing and reconnaissance operations, activation and deployment of assessment personnel or teams, and geospatial and geographic information system support needed for incident management; and, (5) coordinates overall staffing of Federal emergency management activities at multiagency coordination centers. FEMA is also responsible for setting training standards for each individual and team that has a role in emergency response.

ESF-6: Mass Care, Emergency Assistance, Housing, and Human Services

ESF-6 works with response partners at all levels of government, nongovernmental organizations, and the private sector to facilitate the delivery of needed services and assistance. Serving as the ESF-6 Coordinator and Primary Agency, FEMA coordinates the provision of Federal assistance to State, tribal, and local governments in four main areas: mass care, emergency assistance, housing, and human services. The mass care function provides food, shelter, first aid, and collects and provides information on survivors to family members. The emergency assistance function provides for the immediate needs beyond those included in the mass care function. These needs range from providing emergency services for household pets and service animals to providing additional aid and services to special needs populations. The housing function provides financial assistance to help disaster victims repair their existing home or secure other housing accommodations. Finally, the human services function helps disaster survivors recover their non-housing losses and helps them obtain disaster loans, food stamps, crisis counseling,

disaster unemployment, case management, and other Federal and State benefits.

ESF-7: Logistics

ESF-7 provides a comprehensive, national disaster logistics planning, management, and sustainment capability that harnesses the resources of Federal logistics partners, key public and private stakeholders, and nongovernmental organizations to meet the needs of disaster victims and responders. ESF-7, which is coordinated by FEMA and the General Services Administration, encompasses both the logistics management and resource support functions of emergency response. FEMA, serving as the Primary Agency for the logistics management function, works to ensure that Federal emergency responders are able to identify and provide the support needed by State and local officials. ESF-7 manages materials, transportation, and facilities. The General Services Administration, which serves as the Primary Agency for the resource support function, supports Federal agencies and State, tribal, and local governments that need resource support prior to, during, and after incidents requiring a coordinated Federal response. The General Services Administration coordinates the locating, procuring, and issuing of necessary resources to support the Federal emergency response and to ensure public safety.

ESF-8: Public Health

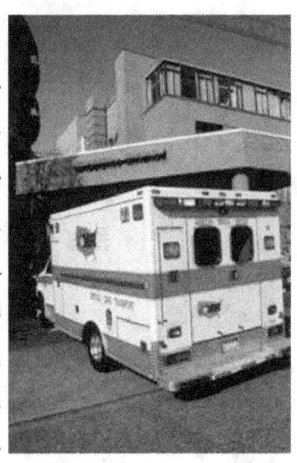

ESF-8 provides the mechanism for coordinated Federal assistance to supplement State, tribal, and local resources in response to a potential or actual public health emergency or natural disaster. ESF-8, which is coordinated by the Department of Health and Human Services, provides a number of health and medical assistance services, including behavior health needs, surge capacity of health professionals, evacuations of those seriously ill, and veterinary animal health response.

ESF-9: Search and Rescue

ESF-9 provides specialized lifesaving assistance to State, tribal, and local authorities when activated for incidents or potential incidents requiring a coordinated Federal response. ESF-9 provides the skills necessary to conduct structural collapse

(urban), waterborne, inland/wilderness, and aeronautical search and rescue operations. FEMA serves as the ESF-9 Coordinator and the Primary Agency for a structural collapse (urban) search and rescue operation. DHS' U.S. Coast Guard serves as the Primary

Agency for a waterborne search and rescue mission. The Department of the Interior's National Park Service acts as the Primary Agency for inland/wilderness search and rescue operations. Finally, the Department of Defense's U.S. Air Force acts as the Primary Agency for aeronautical search and rescue missions.

ESF-10: Oil and Hazardous Materials Response

ESF-10 provides the mechanism for coordinated Federal assistance to supplement State, tribal, and local resources in response to a potential or actual discharge of oil and/or an uncontrolled release of hazardous materials. ESF-10 responses are based upon the National Oil and Hazardous Substances Pollution and Contingency Plan. The Environmental Protection Agency serves as the ESF-10 Coordinator, as well as the Primary Agency for incidents involving inland areas. In addition, the Environmental Protection Agency takes appropriate actions to prepare for, prevent, minimize, and mitigate the threat posed by hazardous materials. DHS' U.S. Coast Guard serves as the Primary Agency for incidents affecting coastal zone areas.

Appendix B

Emergency Support Function Overview

ESF-11: Agriculture and Natural Resources

ESF-11 provides Agriculture and Natural Resources support to States, tribes, and other Federal agencies during disasters and emergencies. Coordinated by the U.S. Department of Agriculture, ESF-11 supports State, tribal, and local authorities and other Federal agency efforts to address: (1) nutrition assistance, (2) protection of natural and cultural resources and historic properties, (3) response to animal/plant diseases and pests, (4) safety and security of commercial food supply, and (5) safety and well-being of household pets.

ESF-12: Energy

ESF-12 facilitates the restoration of damaged energy systems and components. ESF-12, coordinated by the Department of Energy, coordinates Federal, State, local, and private sector efforts to maintain a continuous and reliable source of energy. ESF-12 fosters cooperation between the energy industry and Federal, State, tribal, and local governments to develop and implement methodologies and standards for physical, operational, and cyber security for the energy industry. Following an incident, ESF-12: 1) provides information concerning the energy restoration process, 2) facilitates the restoration of energy systems through legal authorities and waivers, and, 3) provides technical expertise to the utilities, conducts

field assessments, and assists government and private sector stakeholders to overcome challenges in restoring energy systems.

ESF-13: Public Safety and Security

ESF-13 integrates Federal public safety and security capabilities and resources to support the full range of incident management activities associated with potential or actual incidents requiring a coordinated Federal response. Coordinated by the Department of Justice, ESF-13 is activated in situations requiring extensive public safety and security and where State, tribal, and local government resources are overwhelmed or are inadequate. Additionally, ESF-13 can provide protective solutions or capabilities unique to the Federal Government. ESF-13's support capacity includes not only general law enforcement assistance, but also technical support, force protection, and critical infrastructure protection.

ESF-14: Long-Term Community Recovery

ESF-14 provides a mechanism for coordinating Federal support to State, tribal, regional, and local governments, nongovernmental organizations, and the private sector to enable community recovery

Emergency Support Function Overview

from the long-term consequences of extraordinary disasters. Coordinated by FEMA, ESF-14 facilitates a collaboration process to lay the groundwork for wise decisions about the appropriate use of resources and the rebuilding efforts. ESF-14, through its four Primary Agencies—the Department of Agriculture, DHS, the Department of Housing and Urban Development, and the Small Business Administration—provides the funding and expertise to handle challenges such as the redevelopment and reconstruction of communities.

ESF-15: External Affairs

ESF-15 ensures that sufficient Federal assets are deployed to the field during incidents requiring a coordinated Federal response to provide accurate, coordinated, timely, and accessible information to affected audiences, including governments, media, the private sector, and the local populace, including

the special needs population. ESF-15, which is coordinated by DHS, integrates Public Affairs, Congressional Affairs, Intergovernmental Affairs, Com-

munity Relations, and the private sector under the coordinating auspices of External Affairs. Additionally, FEMA, serving as the ESF-15 Primary Agency, provides resources such as the Emergency Alert System, Mobile Emergency Response Support, and the National Preparedness Network.

Appendix C

Inspection Design Matrix

ESF Coordinator						
Researchable Questions	**Information Required**	**Information Sources**	**Data Collection Methods**	**Data Analysis Methods**	**Limitations**	**What Analysis Allows You To Say**
(1) To what extent and in what manner do you coordinate with other Coordinating, Primary and Support Agencies (a) before an incident (including pre-incident planning), (b) during an incident, and (c) after an incident?	Evidence that meetings are being held between ESF Coordinator, Primary Agency, and Support Agency officials to coordinate efforts before, during, and after an incident Evidence that pre-incident plans have been developed or are being developed for potential incidents	ESF Coordinator officials Primary and Support Agency officials National Response Framework • Relevant ESF Annexes • National Planning Scenarios • NRF Incident Annexes	Interviews with cognizant officials Document requests	Analysis of interviews to determine if officials are coordinating with each other during all phases of incident management Document review to corroborate information from interviews and identify information discussed during meetings	Limited cooperation from participating departments and agencies Availability and suitability of documentation to serve as evidence	Extent to which ESF Coordinator, Primary Agency, and Support Agency officials are coordinating with each other during all phases of incident management Extent to which pre-incident plans have been completed and implemented
(2) To what extent do you coordinate with private sector organizations to identify and maximize use of private sector resources in response to a threat or incident?	Evidence that meetings are being held between ESF Coordinator, Primary Agency, and private sector organizations to coordinate how all available resources will be utilized in response to an incident	ESF Coordinator officials Primary and Support Agency officials Appropriate private sector officials National Response Framework • Relevant ESF Annexes • Private Sector Coordination Support Annex	Interviews with cognizant officials Document Requests	Analysis of interviews to determine if Federal government officials are coordinating with corresponding private sector organizations Document review to corroborate information from interviews and identify information discussed during meetings	Limited cooperation from participating departments and agencies Availability and suitability of documentation to serve as evidence	Extent to which ESF Coordinator and Primary Agency officials are coordinating their efforts with private sector organizations in maximizing the use of all available resources
(3) To what extent do you coordinate ESF activities for catastrophic incident planning (e.g., National Planning Scenarios) and critical infrastructure preparedness, as appropriate?	Evidence that ESF Coordinator and Primary Agency officials are coordinating activities for catastrophic incident planning and critical infrastructure preparedness	ESF Coordinator officials Primary Agency officials National Response Framework • Incident Annexes • National Planning Scenarios	Interviews with cognizant officials Document requests	Analysis of interviews and documents to determine if officials are coordinating ESF activities for incident planning and infrastructure preparedness Reviewing meeting agenda papers, meeting minutes, and other documents as necessary	Limited cooperation from participating departments and agencies Availability and suitability of documentation to serve as evidence	Extent to which ESF Coordinator and Primary Agency officials coordinate ESF activities for catastrophic incident planning and critical infrastructure preparedness

Appendix C

Inspection Design Matrix

ESF Primary Agency

Researchable Questions	Information Required	Information Sources	Data Collection Methods	Data Analysis Methods	Limitations	What Analysis Allows You To Say
(1) To what extent and in what manner do you coordinate with the ESF Coordinator, Primary and Support agency officials, State officials, State operations centers, State agencies, and the private sector?	Evidence that Primary Agency officials coordinate with the ESF Coordinator, other Primary and Support Agency officials, State officials, State operations centers, State agencies, and the private sector	ESF Coordinator Primary Agency officials State officials Operations centers officials State Agency officials Private sector officials	Interviews with cognizant officials Document requests	Analysis of interviews to provide descriptive analysis of coordination	Limited cooperation from participating departments and agencies Availability and suitability of documentation to serve as evidence	Extent to which Primary Agency officials coordinate with the ESF Coordinator, other Primary and Support Agency officials, State officials, operations centers, State agencies, and the private sector
(2) To what extent are you prepared to provide trained staff for operations functions, such as supporting interagency emergency response and support teams, at fixed and field facilities?	Evidence that Primary Agency has identified and is prepared to provide trained personnel to support interagency emergency response and support teams at fixed and field facilities	Primary Agency officials Relevant ESF Annexes	Interviews with cognizant officials Document requests	Analysis of interviews and documents to identify trained and credentialed personnel assigned to support interagency emergency response and support teams Analysis of interviews and documents, including a list of employees that primary agency has assigned to fixed and field facilities, if needed	Limited cooperation from participating departments and agencies Availability and suitability of documentation to serve as evidence	Extent to which Primary Agency is prepared to provide trained staff for operations functions, such as supporting interagency emergency response and support teams, at fixed and field facilities
(3) To what extent and in what manner do you conduct situational and periodic readiness assessments? How often have they been coordinated, and how have findings been applied?	Evidence that Primary Agency conducts situational and periodic readiness assessments Evidence that assessment findings are applied	Primary Agency officials Readiness Assessments Exercises and drills	Interviews with cognizant officials Document requests	Analysis of interviews and documents to provide descriptive analysis of readiness assessments	Limited cooperation from participating departments and agencies Availability and suitability of documentation to serve as evidence	Extent to which Primary Agency has conducted situational and periodic readiness assessments Extent to which Primary Agency has applied assessment findings

Appendix C

Inspection Design Matrix

ESF Primary Agency						
Researchable Questions	Information Required	Information Sources	Data Collection Methods	Data Analysis Methods	Limitations	What Analysis Allows You To Say
(4) To what extent have you identified new equipment or capabilities required to prevent or respond to new or emerging threats and hazards, or to improve the ability to address existing threats?	Evidence that Primary Agency identifies new equipment or capabilities Evidence that Primary Agency shared this information with the ESF Coordinator, other Primary Agencies, and Support Agencies, as appropriate	Primary Agency officials Training tracking sheets Response asset inventory	Interviews with cognizant officials Document requests	Analysis of interviews and documents to provide descriptive analysis of equipment and capabilities	Limited cooperation from participating departments and agencies Availability and suitability of documentation to serve as evidence	Extent to which Primary Agency has identified new equipment or capabilities needed Extent to which Primary Agency has shared this information with the ESF Coordinator, other Primary Agencies, and Support Agencies
(5) To what extent have you executed contracts and procured goods and services needed to fulfill your ESF role?	Evidence that Primary Agency executes contracts and procures goods and services Evidence that contracts are properly executed	Primary Agency officials Contracts Purchase orders Independent contracting specialist	Interviews with cognizant officials Document requests	Analysis of interviews and contracts to provide descriptive analysis of procurement practices	Limited cooperation from participating departments and agencies Availability and suitability of documentation to serve as evidence	Extent to which Primary Agency has executed contracts and procured goods and services as needed Extent to which Primary Agency properly executed contracts to ensure goods and services were received as needed
(6) To what extent are you prepared to manage mission assignments and ensure financial and property accountability for ESF activities?	Evidence that Primary Agency is managing mission assignments and ensuring financial and property accountability for ESF activities	Primary Agency officials Mission assignment personnel NRF Financial Support Annex Cooperative Agreement and/or Memorandum of Understanding with FEMA	Interviews with cognizant officials Document requests (such as guidance provided to mission assignment participants on expectations, roles, and responsibilities)	Analysis of interviews and documents to identify examples of Primary Agency officials effectively managing mission assignments Analysis of interviews and documents to provide descriptive analysis of accountability practices	Limited cooperation from participating departments and agencies Availability and suitability of documentation to serve as evidence	Extent to which Primary Agency is prepared to manage mission assignments and ensure financial and property accountability for ESF activities

Appendix C

Inspection Design Matrix

ESF Primary Agency						
Researchable Questions	**Information Required**	**Information Sources**	**Data Collection Methods**	**Data Analysis Methods**	**Limitations**	**What Analysis Allows You To Say**
(7) To what extent do you plan for short- and long-term incident management and recovery operations?	Evidence that Primary Agency has plans for short- and long-term incident management and recovery operations	Primary Agency officials Short- and long-term recovery plans National Response Framework Volunteer and Donations Management Support Annex	Interviews with cognizant officials Document requests	Analysis of interviews and plans to provide descriptive analysis of planning for short- and long-term incident management and recovery operations	Limited cooperation from participating departments and agencies Availability and suitability of documentation to serve as evidence	Extent to which Primary Agency plans for short- and long-term incident management and recovery operations

Appendix C

Inspection Design Matrix

ESF Support Agency						
Researchable Questions	Information Required	Information Sources	Data Collection Methods	Data Analysis Methods	Limitations	What Analysis Allows You To Say
(1) To what extent have you identified trained personnel, equipment, or other resource support to conduct operations when requested by DHS or the designated ESF Primary Agency?	Evidence that Support Agency has identified trained personnel, equipment, or other resource support to conduct operations	Support Agency officials List of available credentialed personnel, equipment, and other resources to support response	Interviews with cognizant officials Document requests	Analysis of interviews and documents to provide descriptive analysis of trained personnel, equipment, and resources	Limited cooperation of participating departments and agencies Availability and suitability of documentation to serve as evidence	Extent to which Support Agency identifies trained personnel, equipment, or other resource support to conduct operations
(2) To what extent do you participate in planning for short- and long-term incident management and recovery operations and the development of supporting operational plans?	Evidence that Support Agency participates in planning for short- and long-term incident management and recovery operations and the development of supporting operational plans	Support Agency officials Incident management and recovery operations documents, such as Standard Operating Procedures, checklists, or other job aids Operational/ Tactical plans	Interviews with cognizant officials Document requests	Analysis of interviews and documents to provide a descriptive analysis of Support Agency's participation in planning for short- and long-term incident management and recovery operations and the development of supporting operational plans	Limited cooperation of participating departments and agencies Availability and suitability of documentation to serve as evidence	Extent to which Support Agency participates in planning for short- and long-term incident management and recovery operations and the development of supporting operational plans
(3) To what extent do you assist in the conduct of situational assessments and provide input to periodic readiness assessments? How often have they been coordinated, and how have findings been applied?	Evidence that Support Agency assists in the conduct of situational assessments and provides input to periodic readiness assessments Evidence that assessment findings are applied	Support Agency officials Situational and readiness assessments Exercises and drills	Interviews with cognizant officials Document requests	Analysis of interviews and documents to provide a descriptive analysis of Support Agency's participation in situational and readiness assessments	Limited cooperation of participating departments and agencies Availability and suitability of documentation to serve as evidence	Extent to which Support Agency assists in the conduct of situational assessments and periodic readiness assessments Extent to which Support Agency applies assessment findings

Appendix C

Inspection Design Matrix

ESF Support Agency						
Researchable Questions	**Information Required**	**Information Sources**	**Data Collection Methods**	**Data Analysis Methods**	**Limitations**	**What Analysis Allows You To Say**
(4) To what extent do you identify new equipment or capabilities required to prevent or respond to new or emerging threats and hazards or to improve the ability to address existing threats?	Evidence that Support Agency identifies new equipment or capabilities required to prevent or respond to new or emerging threats and hazards, or to improve the ability to address existing threats	Support Agency officials Purchase orders Training tracking sheets	Interviews with cognizant officials Document requests	Analysis of interviews and documents to provide descriptive analysis of equipment and capabilities required to prevent or respond to new or emerging threats and hazards, or to improve the ability to address existing threats	Limited cooperation of participating departments and agencies Availability and suitability of documentation to serve as evidence	Extent to which Support Agency identifies new equipment or capabilities required to prevent or respond to new or emerging threats and hazards or to improve the ability to address existing threats

Appendix D

Internet Resources

- National Planning Scenarios
  http://www.dhs.gov/xlibrary/assets/National_Preparedness_Guidelines.pdf

- National Response Framework
  http://www.fema.gov/pdf/emergency/nrf/nrf-ore.pdf

  - National Response Framework ESF Annex Introduction
    http://www.fema.gov/pdf/emergency/nrf/nrf-esf-intro.pdf

  - National Response Framework ESF-1 Annex
    http://www.fema.gov/pdf/emergency/nrf/nrf-esf-01.pdf

  - National Response Framework ESF-2 Annex
    http://www.fema.gov/pdf/emergency/nrf/nrf-esf-02.pdf

  - National Response Framework ESF-3 Annex
    http://www.fema.gov/pdf/emergency/nrf/nrf-esf-03.pdf

  - National Response Framework ESF-4 Annex
    http://www.fema.gov/pdf/emergency/nrf/nrf-esf-04.pdf

  - National Response Framework ESF-5 Annex
    http://www.fema.gov/pdf/emergency/nrf/nrf-esf-05.pdf

  - National Response Framework ESF-6 Annex
    http://www.fema.gov/pdf/emergency/nrf/nrf-esf-06.pdf

  - National Response Framework ESF-7 Annex
    http://www.fema.gov/pdf/emergency/nrf/nrf-esf-07.pdf

  - National Response Framework ESF-8 Annex
    http://www.fema.gov/pdf/emergency/nrf/nrf-esf-08.pdf

  - National Response Framework ESF-9 Annex
    http://www.fema.gov/pdf/emergency/nrf/nrf-esf-09.pdf

Appendix D

Internet Resources

- ◆ National Response Framework ESF-10 Annex
  http://www.fema.gov/pdf/emergency/nrf/nrf-esf-10.pdf

- ◆ National Response Framework ESF-11 Annex
  http://www.fema.gov/pdf/emergency/nrf/nrf-esf-11.pdf

- ◆ National Response Framework ESF-12 Annex
  http://www.fema.gov/pdf/emergency/nrf/nrf-esf-12.pdf

- ◆ National Response Framework ESF-13 Annex
  http://www.fema.gov/pdf/emergency/nrf/nrf-esf-13.pdf

- ◆ National Response Framework ESF-14 Annex
  http://www.fema.gov/pdf/emergency/nrf/nrf-esf-14.pdf

- ◆ National Response Framework ESF-15 Annex
  http://www.fema.gov/pdf/emergency/nrf/nrf-esf-15.pdf

- ◆ National Response Framework Critical Infrastructure and Key Resources Annex
  http://www.fema.gov/pdf/emergency/nrf/nrf-support-cikr.pdf

- ◆ National Response Framework Private Sector Coordination Annex
  http://www.fema.gov/pdf/emergency/nrf/nrf-support-private.pdf

- ◆ National Response Framework Catastrophic Incident Annex
  http://www.fema.gov/pdf/emergency/nrf/nrf_CatastrophicIncidentAnnex.pdf

- ◆ National Response Framework Financial Management Support Annex
  http://www.fema.gov/pdf/emergency/nrf/nrf-support-fin.pdf

- Mission Assignment Billing and Reimbursement Checklist
  http://www.fema.gov/government/billinst.shtm

- Emergency Management Institute Independent Study 293: Mission Assignment Overview
  http://training.fema.gov/EMIWeb/IS/is293.asp